WHO AM I?

I am strong and stripy, fast and fierce.
I live in the jungle.

WHO AM I?

By Moira Butterfield
Illustrated by Wayne Ford

Belitha Press

First Published in the UK in 1996 by

Belitha Press Limited, London House,
Great Eastern Wharf, Parkgate Road,
London SW11 4NQ

ISBN 1 85561 571 1 (hardback)
ISBN 1 85561 581 9 (paperback)

British Library in Cataloguing in Publication Data for this book
is available from the British Library.

Printed in Hong Kong

Editor: Jilly MacLeod
Designer: Helen James
Illustrator: Wayne Ford / Wild Life Art Agency
Consultant: Andrew Branson

I am furry, big and strong.

My teeth are sharp.

My tail is long.

My coat is striped.

My eyes are bright.

I am a hunter in the night.

Who am I?

Here is my eye

I see well in the dark so I hunt at night. Can you spot my golden eyes shining in the shadows?

At night I creep through the trees looking for animals to eat. I can see a wild pig and a deer. Can you?

Here are my teeth

My teeth are as sharp as kitchen knives. The longest, sharpest ones are near the front. Can you see them?

When I see a tasty animal I chase after it and jump on to its back. Then I kill it with my sharp teeth.

Here are my claws

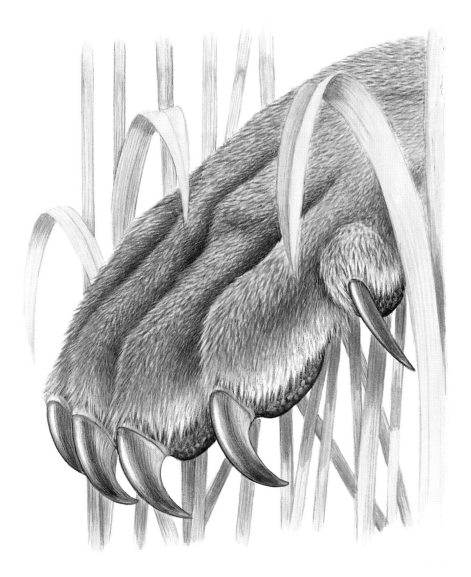

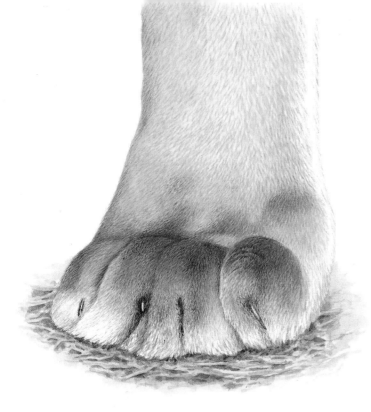

I can hide my claws away in my big furry toes or make them pop out. They are as pointed as needles.

I have four paws. They are soft and padded underneath like cushions. I walk very, very quietly.

Here is my fur

It is orange with black stripes. My colour makes me hard to see when I creep through the bushes.

In the daytime it is too hot to hunt. I lie down and sleep in the long cool grass, out of the sun's heat.

Here are my ears

I can hear every sound. I can even hear a monkey swinging in the trees above my head.

If the monkey sees me he will make lots of noise to warn his friends that I am close by.

Here is my tongue

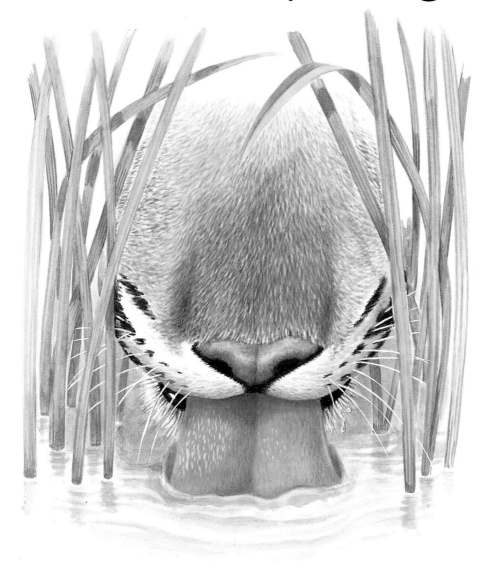

See how long it is.
It feels rough and
knobbly. I lick my
fur clean with my
tongue every day.

I use my tongue to
drink from the river.
I had better watch
out for crocodiles.
Can you see any?

Here is my tail

You can tell when I am angry because my tail lashes to and fro and my long white whiskers stick up.

Then I open my mouth and…

roar!

Have you guessed who I am?

I am a tiger

Point to my...

yellow eyes

pointed ears

padded paws

stripy fur

white whiskers

long tail

I am called a
Bengal tiger

Here are my babies

They are called cubs, and I am their mother. I will look after my cubs until they are big and strong.

My cubs love to play. This cub is chasing a butterfly. One day my cubs will be able to hunt like me.

Here is my home

I live in and around the jungle.

Look for me in the picture. Can you see two little monkeys, three spotted deer, a snake and an elephant as well?

Here is a map
of the world

I live in a hot
country called
India. Where is it
on the map?

Can you point to
the place where
you live?

India

Can you answer these questions about me?

How many paws do I have?

What are my babies called?

Do I like to eat meat?

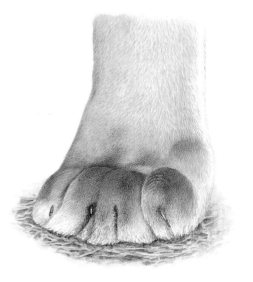

Do I hunt in the daytime or at night?

What noise do I make when I am angry?

Where do I like to sleep when I am hot?

How sharp are my teeth?

What colour is my fur?

Can I see in the dark?

How do I keep my beautiful fur clean?

Here are some words to learn about me

claws My sharp pointed nails. They are curved and they can scratch and tear.

creep This is what I do when I move very quietly and slowly along the ground. I creep when I am hunting.

cub The name for one of my babies.

fur My soft warm coat. It is orange with black stripes.

knobbly Lumpy and bumpy, like my tongue.

roar The loud noise I make. Can you roar like me?

teeth I use my sharp teeth for biting and chewing. They are much sharper and bigger than your teeth.

tongue I use my tongue for licking and tasting. Mine is much bigger and rougher than yours.

whiskers Fine hairs that sprout out from my cheeks. They stick up when I am angry.